AND NOW WHAT?

Steps to Take When a Loved One Is Considering Downsizing and Moving

A Guide Through All Stages of the Process

JENNIFER TAYLOR

Published by
Jennifer Taylor
KANSAS CITY, MO
ClearItOutKC.com

ISBN: 979-8-218-63898-6

Production: Gary A. Rosenberg • www.thebookcouple.com

Contents

Introduction

This guide has been developed by someone who has helped thousands of individuals through the process of downsizing since 2009.

My name is Jennifer Taylor, and I live in Parkville, Missouri. In 2009, I founded my company Clear It Out because I realized there was a real need to help people with the process of downsizing and moving. I obtained my real estate license in 2015 to further assist people who requested my services, and I have helped thousands of people through the years in the Kansas City metropolitan area.

Through my experience, I learned something that surprised me. I noticed people frequently stayed in their homes longer than was safe because they didn't know how to start the process of downsizing and moving. Building on my years of experience in this field, I have learned the most effective ways to help clients with sorting, packing, moving, and disposing of unnecessary possessions.

This book gives you guidance through these steps and more. I also include senior living options that exist and tips on selling the family home. Not all suggestions will work for everyone, but my hope is that you find some information to make the process go as smoothly as possible for you and your loved one(s).

The Process of Moving or Downsizing Is Unique to Every Person

The topic of when, where, and how to downsize and/or move is something everyone will face at one time or another, and every situation is different. Whether it be family support, finances, or even local resources, the factors that should be considered when someone needs to move from their home will vary with each family. The situation is not only physically draining, but it can also be overwhelming and mentally exhausting. You need to take the process one step at a time. In my years of helping people with this process, I have observed and assisted with the many options that could be available for your family. This book will provide an overview of them and guidance as to what may work best for your situation.

CHAPTER 1

How to Know When
the Time Is Right:
If You Can Ever Be Sure

It can be very difficult to know when it is time for you or an aging loved one to move from a current home. If you haven't been there yet, you will be at some point. Whether it's yourself or a grandparent, aunt, uncle, parent, sibling, or even a friend, you may wonder, "Are they okay living on their own?" or "Would my loved one do better being around people every day?" Loneliness and lack of socialization are very large areas of concern in the elderly population. You might notice that sometimes your loved one does not care for themselves very effectively. They may forget to bathe, take medication, or eat or be unsafe trying to maneuver stairs in their home. They may struggle with simple home upkeep tasks. Sometimes they might even leave home and struggle to find their way back.

Throughout this book, I will share stories of

people I encountered while helping them with their moving needs, in case the real-life examples are useful to you. Here is the first one:

> *I had a client who left her home during a snowstorm to attend morning mass at 6:30 a.m. It was much earlier than 6:30 a.m. when she arrived in the dark parking lot where mass had been cancelled because of the weather that day. The person clearing the parking lot noticed her and made sure she returned home safely. That was a happy ending; however, some endings do not have such positive outcomes.*

When an incident like this occurs, Silver Alerts are issued. A Silver Alert is a public notification system to alert people to missing persons—in particular, senior citizens with memory issues. People can be found hours away from home, but sometimes when they are found, it is too late.

How Many Needs Does Your Aging Loved One Have?

If you are helping to take care of an aging loved one, have you ever stopped to think about how much time you are spending on their care? Have you had to cut back on hours or stop working altogether to meet their needs? Caregivers spend time running errands, shopping, making sure their loved ones have their prescriptions and are taking them correctly, doing lawn work, checking in on them with a phone call, handling their financial affairs, or taking them to appointments. If you just made a note either mentally or on paper of all that you do for your aging loved one, I'm willing to bet you spend more time on their needs than you originally thought!

Financial Scams That Target the Aging Population

Another area of concern regards financial issues with your aging loved one. There are people who prey on the elderly. Some of the schemes well known for trying to extort money from the elderly are:

- Sweepstakes/lottery schemes—a scammer tells your loved one that they "won" a sweepstakes or lottery but need to submit a payment before the proceeds are mailed.

- Car warranty purchase—I've had clients who paid for an extended car warranty on a car that they no longer owned.

- "Grandchild" that needs help—with the invention of artificial intelligence (AI), a call can be made to your loved one with a voice that may sound just like their grandchild, niece, nephew, and so forth; frequently, the scammer requests money to "help" them.

- Government and banking schemes—a person may call and request information, such as a social security number, bank account information, or passwords in order to gain access to your loved one's money.

- Email phishing—a scammer sends an email to acquire your loved one's sensitive data; the email may have a link that if clicked on looks legitimate, but it is not. It is an attempt to acquire information.

- Computer support scheme—this is when a victim's computer appears to have a virus, and they are directed to call a number on the screen. When they do, sensitive information is requested and, frequently, control of the computer is compromised.

These kinds of scams can and will happen to aging loved ones, and they could happen to someone you know. Some of my friends have dealt with these situations firsthand:

I had a friend whose mother gave $50,000 to a Jamaican lottery scheme. It was basically her life savings. Her family only found out after she asked her daughter for an additional $40,000. She was *angry at her family for interfering in her getting the $1,000,000 and BMW that she had "won" in the fake lottery.*

I had another friend whose mother received a call from someone who said it was their grandson and a supposed attorney. The grandson was supposedly in jail in another state and needed $3,000 in bail money. The grandmother went to wire bail money to help her grandson. Needless to say, her grandson was safely located in the same city as her. She never recovered the money.

A credit freeze is a good way to help stop someone from opening an account in your loved one's name. In fact, it is a great idea for everyone. A credit freeze blocks access to a person's credit report, which may prevent scammers from accessing it and opening additional lines of credit. It does not prevent them from using a social security number in other unauthorized ways. However, it may prevent the opening of unauthorized accounts.

Medical Guidance May Help Your Decision

It may be important to get your loved one's physician involved in a decision regarding their care. You should attend their appointments to be their ears and their advocate.

QUESTIONS TO ASK YOURSELF

It may never be easy or simple to encourage your aging loved one to move, but here are some questions that may help clarify matters after you have considered the demands on your time, financial issues, and medical advice. Keep in mind that your aging loved ones should be around people and have opportunities to socialize as well as have their basic needs met.

❑ What events around them could help with this?

❑ Are there community centers nearby they can attend that will help keep their mind active?

❑ Is there a senior center nearby for meals and socialization?

❑ Does a meal delivery service exist if cooking is a problem?

Even if you feel that your aging loved one should no longer live alone, they may not agree, and you may not have much say in the situation. The best scenario is when people can make the decision on their own versus someone else making the decision for them. The transition will go much smoother and will be better when they feel they are still involved.

CHAPTER 2

The Emotional Toll

If you have been through the process of moving or downsizing an aging loved one before or know someone who has, you know what an emotional toll it can take on a person or family. When material possessions or money come into play, people can change. I've also been in situations where people who have memory issues can become very upset with the process. They feel like they are losing control, and sometimes they say things that can be hurtful even if they don't really mean it. For example:

> I had a client a few years ago who moved their spouse to an assisted living community. His wife's cognitive ability had declined significantly and that was the reason for the move. He chose to have an estate sale at their home and brought his wife to the estate sale. She was confused and very upset with what was happening. She became angry and belligerent with her husband. According to people who knew her, that was not her personality at all.

It seems that there is always one person in a family who does most of the work. It might be because they live closer to the person, have more experience, or have more time in their schedule. It is important to acknowledge that person for the work they are doing. Even if they volunteer to do it, it can be emotionally draining. For example:

I had a client with three children, and only one lived locally. That child took on the majority of responsibility caring for my client. The out-of-town siblings wanted to help, but with jobs and young children, they could not physically be there to help. The in-town sibling needed the other siblings to recognize how much work it was to care for their parent and help with what they could, even if was making phone calls and traveling to help when they were able.

In my professional role, I have done a lot of hand-holding figuratively and literally through the years. I have seen a lot of tears from both clients and family members. Seeking emotional support for those helping the family member through the process may be necessary.

CHAPTER 3

Options to Help You with an Aging Loved One's Care: Could a Nurse Case Manager or Guardianship Help?

For those who want to help an aging loved one and are not concerned about their living alone, there are options. If someone is no longer able to care for themselves or their home properly but may not see it that way themselves, it may be time to talk with their physician to get their support in finding help for your loved one.

It can be difficult to move an aging loved one once their situation has progressed to being untenable, so starting the process even when it seems "too early" can pay off in the long run. I have been called in to help clients once they have been deemed unable to make the decisions for themselves. Frequently, it is a contentious situation since the client doesn't want to start the process of downsizing and/or want to move. I remind people when I have speaking engagements that it is much better when an aging loved one starts the process on their own and can make their own decisions.

Outside help can be useful, and it comes in many forms, which I detail in this chapter. In my capacity as a consultant, I have been able to offer direct and indirect support and guidance in various ways to clients:

I received a phone call one time to help a senior client at an independent living apartment complex. She was vision impaired, however, living in a one-bedroom apartment. She needed help making her apartment safe since she was a hoarder. She was also a smoker. We noticed several burn holes in her bed comforter. We did what we could to improve the safety in her apartment. Later, someone called in her situation to the state. Because my card was located in her apartment, someone from the state senior services division called me to ask my opinion on her living in her apartment alone. I was able to provide objective insight to the case worker to ensure the client's well-being.

A Nurse Case Manager

A nurse case manager may be a valuable asset to you at this time too. Nurse case managers oversee not only the physical but the mental wellness of a client. They work closely with physicians, nurses, mental health practitioners, and other health care professionals, as well as family and friends of clients. Check with your insurance company for recommendations for a nurse case manager. If they are covered by insurance, you may need a referral from a doctor.

Guardianship

If you feel strongly that your loved one is no longer able to make decisions in their best interest, talk to an attorney on how to obtain guardianship for them through the court system. Some attorneys focus on seniors and their unique situations and can assist with planning for their estate. They can prepare necessary paperwork such as a medical power of attorney, a living will, trusts, and asset protection. Check with your attorney or an elder law attorney.

Local Area Agencies on Aging (AAA) are also available to help those sixty years or older, with special emphasis given to low-income clients. AAA came about as a result of the 1973 amendments to the federal Older Americans Act, in which states were required to develop and implement programs and services for older persons at the local level. Some of the services they are required to provide are legal services, nutrition, in-home services such as chores and personal care, disease prevention, health promotion, outreach, and transportation. They may also provide help with taxes, elder rights, health education, recreation, and minor home repairs.

Sometimes, an aging loved one's situation may be flagged by a government agency, which prompts guardianship:

> *I've encountered situations where individuals were "hot lined" to the Department of Health and Senior Services because it was determined that they were no longer safe living in their own home. It may have been the result of a fall that required help for them to get up or when someone entered the home and was concerned about the person's living conditions or their health. In these cases, and after research has been done, guardianship may be assigned.*

If you are too busy or feel it's best to have an impartial person help with an aging loved one, remember an elder law attorney or a nurse case manager may be the answer.

CHAPTER 4

Age in Place or Make a Move?

You may ask yourself when confronted with the realities of an aging loved one whether they should remain living in the home or move. Much of this decision will depend on the individual's health, their financial situation including what they can afford, their resources, and what is available in their location. When you begin to contemplate next steps, consider what they need now, plus what they may need in the future. There also may be a spouse to consider.

Here are a few options to consider for your aging loved one:

- Age in place

- In-home health care and nonmedical in-home care

- Adult day care

- Live with a loved one

- An apartment

- Maintenance-provided community

- Condominium

- Housing cooperative

- Independent-living community

- Continuous care community

- Assisted-living community

- Residential care home

- Veterans Affairs (VA) medical foster home

- Nursing home/skilled nursing home

- Memory care community

I will detail more about each of these choices below.

Age in Place

Age in place may be your aging loved one's first choice if the preference is to stay in the home. This may be possible if the home is a safe environment. As a person ages, costs for hiring help may increase. This may include people to:

- Clean

- Take care of the lawn and snow removal

- Do general home maintenance

Your aging loved one may want to consider aging in place by selling the larger family home and purchasing a smaller home. They may also get to a point where they need to hire in-home care for personal needs as I detail below.

However, keep costs in mind and encourage your aging loved one to consider all factors in their decision making. Aging in place may become more complicated and costly if someone's health declines and they need constant care. For example:

I had a client who I visited with regarding moving. His wife had Parkinson's, which had become progressively worse. She had fallen and recently broken her hip. Although they preferred to age in place and have help come to the home, the cost of the in-home care became exorbitant. Hourly, around the clock care for his wife exceeded $20,000 per month. They were able to move to assisted living together, and it cost significantly less.

In-Home Care

Hiring a company or person for in-home care may be a good idea if the decision is that it is better for your loved one to remain in the home. Home health care usually involves medically trained personnel, while nonmedical home care involves people helping with meals, housekeeping, bathing, reminders to take medications, errands, or companionship.

The amount you pay for in-home care will vary and depend on if the home care is medical or not. Search reviews on companies in your area and rely on personal references when available. It might be necessary to interview more than one company or caregiver because you want a good relationship between your loved one and their caregiver. If you choose to hire an individual, go through the same steps a company would go through. Make sure the individual is licensed and insured and complete a credit and background check on them.

Adult Day Care

If you or your loved one is not quite ready to commit to a move, or your chosen facility has a waiting list, adult day care might be an option. Adult day care provides the caregiver a break. The caregiver may choose to spend time running errands or doing things they enjoy. Whatever they choose, adult day care gives them a mental and physical break from their caregiving duties, and they can be assured that their loved one's needs are being met.

Live with a Loved One

If you think you would like to move your aging loved one in with you, that can be easier said than done. What is their need for their own space, and can that be provided? You must be prepared for the unexpected things that go along with this option. It should save you money, but it will require patience and potentially some remodeling. If you have steps and your loved one has difficulty maneuvering steps, you will need to find a way to accommodate that situation. You may need to remodel a bathroom for a zero-clearance entry into a shower. If your loved one is suffering from dementia, they can get their days and nights switched around. You will need to be prepared to make your home safe for them and find a way to keep them from wandering outside at night while everyone is sleeping.

If you decide you would like to take some time away with other family members, you may be able to locate respite care for your loved one. Respite care is planned or emergency temporary care that can take place in your home or in a residential center that offers adult day care or overnight stays. Some insurance plans may cover respite care, but many do not. You will need to speak with your insurance company to verify.

An Apartment

Apartment living is another option if your family member is able to care for themselves but not really wanting the headache of a home and yard. I've had several clients through the years who moved into a community that prepared meals for them, but they eventually decided that they did not quite need that level of care. They moved out of assisted living and into an apartment. This option may be good, but you should still be aware if your loved one is having to maneuver stairs and if they are able to provide most of the care for themselves.

In many areas of the country, providing meals or food in general is not as big of a concern as it used to be in the past. Some areas provide Meals on Wheels where lunch is delivered four to five days a week. Also, grocery delivery has become an option almost everywhere. Mail order of necessary supplies and food is an option too.

Maintenance-Provided Community

A maintenance-provided community is a good option if it is preferred to maintain independence in a home. Sometimes, the units will have a shared wall with a neighbor. Most of these neighborhoods have homes that are single-level living, and the outside lawn maintenance and snow removal are covered by the homeowner's association (HOA). Sometimes, the roof and painting of the outside of the home are also covered by the HOA. It is important to read the covenants and restrictions for the neighborhood to know what is covered with your HOA fee.

Condominium

Condominiums (condos) are another great option. They are similar to an apartment but are owned by individuals who also have interest in common areas. They will have an HOA fee and may have amenities to go with it. They may offer a workout area, pool, or social area.

Housing Cooperative

Housing cooperatives (co-ops) are available in certain areas of the country. They may appear similar to owning a condo; however, there is one main difference. With a co-op, you own shares in the corporation instead of a specific unit. You also have a say in decisions related to the building but are required to pay for those items decided upon.

Independent-Living Community

Independent living is very similar to living in an apartment. The biggest difference is that in a fifty-five-plus independent living community, the activities are geared toward the age group. As in apartment living, meals, food, and supplies may be ordered for delivery. Most communities have many activities to encourage interaction with others.

Continuing Care Community

Another type of community is a continuing care community (CCRC). This type of community may also be referred to as a life plan community. They provide a continuum of care for individuals from independent living sometimes in a villa, to assisted living, and finally to skilled nursing or memory care as needed by the resident. This may be a good option if a person is able to afford the buy-in. A buy-in fee is what a resident pays that essentially "holds" a spot in the highest level of nursing care available at the community. A higher buy-in fee may result in a lower monthly fee. If there is a home to sell, that may provide the buy-in cost. Besides the buy-in cost, there are monthly fees to pay too. The monthly fees may include costs for long-term care insurance. It may be a required fee even if your loved one already has long-term care insurance.

In this type of community, an aging loved one and their partner may be able to reside at the same community, albeit separately, if one person needs additional care. Because of how these communities function, your loved one will most likely need to provide all of their financial information to the community prior to being accepted to live there. Some CCRCs also have a foundation that people can contribute to. The foundation is set up to assist those who can no longer afford to live in the community. Although people may have financials that show quite a few assets, sometimes things happen, and those financials are not as solid as they think. If considering a CCRC, please ask what could happen if your loved one "runs out of money." Not all aging communities offer CCRCs; however, there definitely is a benefit to not having to move a loved one as additional care becomes necessary.

Assisted-Living Community

Assisted living is a community that provides a balance between a need for support and a desire for independence. Additional care of needed services including meals, housekeeping, laundry, and medication distribution may be found in assisted living. Frequent welfare checks and activities such as social outings and wellness programs should also be included. An assisted-living community can provide peace of mind if you are concerned about your family member living alone.

Several times, I have packed clients who initially moved to assistant living together. When one of them needed additional care, they had to move to another community because their current community did not provide a high enough level of care or they did not have an opening at the time. Later, the client who remained at the first community was able to reserve an apartment where their spouse moved and be under the same roof as them again. One client was lucky enough to have their apartment and their spouse's separated by only one door.

Residential Care Home

In some locations, you might be able to find a residential care home. These function as an assisted living community, but many times they cost less. They can help with personal care, medication, meals, and so forth and are staffed 24/7. There are usually four to ten residents per professional depending on state regulations.

VA Medical Foster Home

The VA Medical Foster Home program is a long-term care option for veterans who need help living on their own. The program offers a home-like setting with a caregiver who provides daily care and supervision. The program aims to treat aging veterans like family.

Skilled Nursing/Respite Care

Skilled nursing communities are sometimes referred to as nursing homes or respite care. They are meant for patients who are rehabbing. They may become a permanent living situation if your loved one does not improve enough to be moved to long-term care. In skilled nursing, residents receive the help of medically trained professionals such as nurses, physical and occupational thera-pists, and speech pathologists and audiologists. Music therapy is another option to potentially help seniors.

Memory Care Community

Memory care communities are a wonderful option for loved ones who have memory issues or for those who have declined in cognition and may be in danger of wandering. These communi-ties also make sure that your loved ones are in a secured environment around the clock; that they eat, bathe, and take medication as prescribed; and that they participate in activities. Memory care communities should provide custom programs to treat memory loss and help your aging loved one recall times of the past via music and activities. Consistency helps keep your loved one calm and comfortable.

How to Decide on Next Steps and What to Do When Your Aging Loved One Needs Increased Care

What happens when your loved one needs additional care that cannot be provided where they currently live? Ultimately, whoever is overseeing the care of a loved one needs to make sure their needs are being met. An option if you and the community agree may be to allow your loved one to remain at the community with additional care such as in-home care added to their daily schedule.

When looking for a community that is a "good fit," search out communities where your loved one currently has friends. Make appointments to visit different communities, have lunch, and participate in some activities. This gives your loved one an opportunity to meet other residents. Another idea would be to ask if your loved one could spend a couple of nights at the community or communities being considered. This too allows them to meet other residents as well as sample the food and try some of the activities.

There are companies that help locate an assisted living or memory care center that are free to you because they are paid by the communities in which they place people. Be sure to ask to see any community you may be interested in even if the company does not recommend it.

Before you make a final decision, ask to see the results of the community's previous state survey. This includes deficiencies that have been noted by state inspectors as well as complaints reported and the outcomes of those investigations. It is possible to locate information online regarding communities.

As with any major decision, please seek legal help if questions exist. The quality of a community may vary from location to location and company to company. Ask questions and do research to make sure what you select is the best option for your loved one.

CHAPTER 5

First Steps to Take When Downsizing and/or Moving

If your aging loved one has been living in their home for an extended time, there may be an attic or basement no one has gone through in a really long time. Where is the best place to start?

If you have the luxury of time, the best thing to do is to make a commitment to work on one small area, closet, or a couple of drawers a week. **Setting a small goal makes the task manageable**. If a plan is made to clean out an entire room in one day, someone may get frustrated, shut the door, and never finish.

Once you set the session's goal, set up four boxes and label them:

1. Trash

2. Donate

3. Sell

4. Shred

If there are things you'd like to keep, put them away as you encounter them.

When finished sorting the closet or drawers, close up the boxes and do not reopen them. Make it a practice to touch things only one time. Items that can be donated or trashed should be moved from the home.

If a family member or company is completing the job, it may go much quicker.

Keep an Eye Out for Hidden Money

One item to keep an eye out for is hidden money. People who lived through the Great Depression may not trust banks, so they hid money within their home. Here are some examples from my own experience:

We were hired by an attorney to clean out a house of clients who had passed away. In that house, we found a bandage tin with nearly $4,000 in it. We also located a lockbox in the workshop downstairs. In that lockbox was approximately $96,000. The money had been damaged by water and had to be sent off to the US Treasury to be counted. We have also had clients hide money in books. While preparing to donate some books for a client, we flipped through the books and $100 bills fell out. The daughter was surprised when we

*handed the money over to her. She had no idea her
mom had hid money in the books.*

Not all people hide money, but it is worth
keeping your eyes open for money when clearing
out a home.

Fairly Distributing Material Objects

If your loved one is moving to independent living
or an apartment, they will need to keep quite a
few of their home contents unless they are moving
to a fully furnished residence. Whether moving to
a furnished apartment or taking their own furniture, once you decide what furniture to keep, the
next step is to sort and pack it. It is at this time that
family members are usually asked to "claim" contents that your aging loved one no longer needs or
wants. A few suggestions for helping to disperse
contents among family members:

1. Sell everything via one of the methods in chap-
    ter 7. I had a client with a blended family that
    decided the fairest way to treat everyone was to
    have everyone purchase what they would like
    to keep.

2. Have someone price items that are not being
    kept and give family members "play" money to
    purchase items they would like to keep.

3. Have a system whereby the youngest or oldest relative picks an item they would like to keep and then do the selection process again, but in reverse.

4. Have a lottery system where relatives draw numbers to see who selects an item first, second, third, and so on.

5. Ask your relatives to make a list of personal items and who gave those items to them. This option allows for the person who gave the gift to have it returned to them if they would like it back.

A set method takes away the feeling of playing favorites. People will frequently ask me, *What has the most value in a home?* I tell people the items with the most value are those that mean the most to you. **Just because something has monetary value does not mean it is important to you**.

Clients tell me that their family members often do not want the items they are trying to hand off to them. Please don't take offense to this. It is just the way it is with the younger generation. They seem to believe that less is more and do not want anything "extra" sitting around. They will take antiques and paint them. They will take china cabinets apart and keep the bottom only as a sideboard in their dining room. If they want something, they usually are repurposing it. As for beautiful china, the younger generation frequently does not want it because they prefer dishes that can go in the dishwasher or paper products that can be thrown away. Ultimately, whatever system works for your family in distributing contents from a loved one's home is what you should do.

Dealing with Memorabilia and Heirloom Items

Another thing to think about is what do you do with a family heirloom, children's artwork, or an item with wonderful memories that you no longer have room for? **Why not take a picture and have a photo book made of those favorite things?** The book could be displayed and shared with people without holding on to the item. For example:

We once worked with a wonderful family in the process of their downsizing and moving. We pulled out a small baby lamp and my client teared up. She informed us that the lamp belonged to her son who had passed away nearly twenty years ago. We suggested she take a picture of the lamp and keep the memory, but not the item. She agreed and was able to donate the lamp to charity. That lamp could now bring happy memories to another family, but our client still could have the memory associated with it.

Determining What Can Be Moved

When your aging loved one decides what they are keeping, someone needs to measure the new home to make sure things they want to take fit and keep your loved one safe. Sometimes it is difficult for family members to part with contents, but ultimately, safety is most important. Contents/furniture at a new residence must be placed where your loved one can maneuver safely within their new residence.

If your aging loved one is able to take large furniture to display favorite items like a curio cabinet with them, it is a good idea to take a picture of the cabinet before it is packed and moved so you can help them place items as they were located in the cabinet as they remember it.

Packing Up

Pack what contents are wanted/needed by you or your aging loved one. Additionally, most moving companies will pack for someone they are moving. Sometimes professional packers are available and may cost less money than traditional movers to pack.

Is your loved one moving a long distance? If so, some people have asked me about the option of portable on-demand storage. This is where a container is dropped off at your loved one's home, you load it, and the company picks it up and takes it where you are moving. There are several companies that offer this service, but you will need to look in your area. This could be a good option as long as you can load the container and/or can find help loading it. Some movers will allow you to hire labor only from them. Make sure to check for hidden fees before committing to any specific on-demand storage company.

Another option, whether your loved one is moving a long distance or just cannot get their contents moved to where they are settling right now, is a storage unit. Sometimes, a loved one needs to go to a rehabilitation center prior to going to their new residence. In this case, have their contents moved to a storage unit until their new residence is ready or they are ready to move in. Even if just moving to assisted living, it may be a kinder option to put items in storage for a loved one if they aren't ready to part with certain things, even if it is more work for you. I would highly suggest climate-controlled storage if you have furniture and valuables that may be damaged by temperature extremes. I also suggest my clients take a look at the storage unit they will be renting to make sure there is no water, insects, and so forth in the storage unit.

Here is something to keep in mind before you settle on a storage unit solution: I believe if you place contents in a storage unit and pay to leave them there for a long period of time, you probably don't need those items anymore.

If your aging loved one is moving across the country, another thing to think about is cost. *Would it be more cost effective to purchase new or pay to have their contents moved?* When working with long-distance movers, we have found that several of them broker the move with local companies to pick up your contents and move them to a storage unit until they can be combined with another move. Keep in mind that multiple moves can create more chances for items to be damaged.

Some companies will rent plastic tubs for moving. This service may exist where you reside, but you will need to search to make sure. It is a good option for those who like to have a "green" option. Inquire about their cleaning/sanitizing of the tubs if you would like to pursue this option.

Selecting Movers

Selecting a moving company in your area should be based on reviews and personal references. Another option for moving just a few items is a service where individuals use their own trucks to move items for people. You *must* review the pros and cons to this option. Traditional movers should have insurance to cover any damage they may cause your residence or contents. Movers who use their own truck may not have insurance to cover those things. However, if you are looking for a reasonable way to move just a few items that are not fragile, it may be a more economical way to go about the move.

Getting Other People's Stuff Out of the Home

Then, there are relatives (often children) who use their aging loved one's home as a storage unit. This happens more often than you might think. I like to tell clients the best way to handle this is to give your family member notice that an aging loved one is moving. As soon as you know they are moving, let your relative know that they need to come get their items.

If you have the luxury of time and the first notice doesn't work, then give them another notice or two. Make sure they know of the move and communicate that their items need to find a new home. If they have stored their items with your loved one for a long time, they may not remember what is there or even care to keep the contents. Whatever you do, do not allow someone else's items to make your loved one stay in the home longer than needed. If family members would like to keep the items, they can pay for a storage unit.

Individual states have laws regarding "abandoned property." You have rights regarding options for that property but will need to consult an attorney where the property is located to know what you can legally do with it.

Here are some examples from my experiences with this situation:

When I was first married, every time I was close to my parents' house, they gave me another box of my "stuff." They were not going to become stuck storing my things.

In another situation, parents had been asking their grown daughter to come get her items for nearly six months. She did not pick them up and they donated her items to charity. The daughter then sued her parents, and she lost in court. That being said, I am not an attorney, so please seek legal advice if needed regarding this topic.

CHAPTER 6

Tips for Packing

Whether your loved one is moving down the street or across the country, packing takes quite a bit of time and supplies to do it correctly. Every drawer, cabinet, and closet needs to be emptied. Many times, people are downsizing and will need to get rid of contents they no longer want or need. In this chapter, I will provide tips to make the process go more smoothly.

1. Get Rid of Things!

I know it's easier said than done, but most times it is needed. I've had clients tell me they haven't seen the back of their closet in thirty years. Chances are if you haven't worn something or used it in the past year, you don't need it.

Here are some quick tips:

- Clothing is one thing many people have too much of and need to pare down.

- Kitchen small appliances and utensils are

another. If you have an item that can be used for multiple jobs, now is the time to "clear out" and get rid of the items used once a year. Yes, I'm speaking about those holiday dishes used just once a year and the food dehydrator used infrequently too!

2. Pack What Is Not Needed in the Near Future

Leave out the needed place settings, silverware, glasses, pots and pans, and so forth. Pack what you can live without and don't need access to right now.

Here are a few tips for packing:

- Use the correct size box so boxes are not too heavy.

- Place scrunched-up packing paper in the bottom of the box to cushion breakables.

- Tape boxes well so they don't fall apart.

- Place heavier items at the bottom of the box.

- Pack plates and platters on their side.

- Label each box. We recommend the top and two additional sides. Label as thoroughly as needed. Use stickers or different colors of tape to know which room a box goes to and if the items inside are fragile.

- Keep in mind that lamp shades usually require their own box; however, they may be "nested" with smaller ones. Label these boxes as ones that should not have other boxes stacked on top of them.

- Mark boxes with liquids with the word UPRIGHT.

- Do not pack flammable items and liquids; they will need to be moved in a personal vehicle since the movers are not allowed to transport them.

- Make sure you label the location the box is being moved to and not necessarily the location the box is coming from. Your loved one may have had a formal dining room in their prior home but not their new home. Where will the items from that room go in their new home?

- Check with your chosen mover about whether clothing may be left in a dresser. Check for small breakables in those drawers, which will need to be wrapped and placed back in the dresser or removed and packed securely in another box.

- Consider how you pack clothes. Clothes in a closet may be placed in a wardrobe box. Several sizes of wardrobe boxes exist for short or long items. If you choose not to invest in wardrobe boxes, clothing may be folded back and forth on a hanger and placed in a medium-sized box.

- Take a few simple steps to move clothing your-self. A bar in the back of your car may be a good option. Or consider a process where you lay out a sheet, lay clothing left on the hanger, and place the items back-to-back on the sheet. Wrap the sheet as if you are wrapping a burrito. One person then carries the sheet from each side.

- Wrap large artwork, mirrors, and floor lamps in a moving blanket and then tape the moving blanket securely. It is important for a mover to see what they are transporting.

- Try custom boxes for large items. Televisions and some large artwork may be packed in television boxes that telescope in order to fit various sizes.

3. Number Your Boxes

If you are worried about a box going missing, you may want to number them and make a spread-sheet with a summary of what is in each box. This may be particularly useful if your aging loved one is moving a far distance, as their possessions could be shuffled around more significantly. Numbering boxes may also be useful if a move is contentious:

We had a client who was overseeing the distri-bution of contents at a home. The particular con-tents were in a dispute between the person who used to live at the home and his ex-girlfriend. We had to document, photograph, and pack each box and then build a spreadsheet of the boxes and what was in them. That spreadsheet was over 90 pages long!

4. Pack Last-Minute Items in a Box and Transport Them Yourself

Of particular importance are medication and personal items. I also recommend hand-carrying valuables such as jewelry and irreplacable possessions. If your aging loved one has pets, you will need to transport them as well as their food, bed, and comfort objects.

5. Pack an Overnight Bag with a Change of Clothing

Your aging loved one may not feel like unpacking so it's important to have access to a change of clothing for the day of the move.

6. Don't Move What You Don't Need

Moving contents can be expensive. Consider selling items or donating them instead of moving them, especially a long distance. It may be cheaper to replace those items than to move them.

CHAPTER 7

What to Do with Contents That Are No Longer Needed or Wanted

Most times, clients will have contents remaining in their homes even after they move and family members have taken what they would like to keep. Depending on where you live, many options may exist for what to do with those contents. You may also try a combination of the suggestions listed below.

- Your own sale

- Estate sale

- Online estate sale

- Estate buyout

- Auction at the home

- Online auction

- Auction house

- Specialized auction

- Consignment store

- Swap and shops/Facebook Marketplace/ Craigslist

- Donation

- Trash

Let's explore these options in further detail.

Your Own Sale

If you prefer to sell items on your own to keep all of the profit, you may enlist the help of a person to help you set up and price a sale. There are people willing to do this for an hourly charge. I've encountered individuals who do estate sales who may be willing to do this too. I would be careful of calling the event a garage, yard, or tag sale because expectations for someone attending one of those sales is that everything will be cheap. A true downsizing sale contains nice usable items that will not necessarily be priced inexpensively.

Estate Sale

An estate sale is a great way to get rid of many items within a few days. For those of you who have never attended an estate sale, I like to refer to them as a sale throughout the home. Companies that hold these sales come in and price everything in the home. For many companies, this includes half-empty cleaning supplies, unexpired canned goods, tools, clothing, furniture, and just about everything else in the home. They then advertise the sale and conduct the sale between one and three days. The length of time depends on how much there is to sell. Usually on the second or third day, prices are discounted 25% and then 50%.

When nearing the end of the sale, some companies allow for individuals to gather several items and make an offer. This is a great way to move a lot of contents in a quick manner. In order to have an estate sale, you must retain ownership of the home during the sale and keep insurance on the home. It is also ideal for the family to have taken what they want prior to interviewing an estate sale company. That way the estate sale company can evaluate if there are enough items and/or enough value to warrant a sale. The company will keep a percentage of the sale in return for their work. Some companies also have a guaranteed minimum they must make for helping with a sale. This information should be provided prior to you agreeing to work with them.

Some people do not prefer estate sales because they do not feel comfortable having people walk through their home. If this is the case, an estate sale may not be an acceptable option for you. Another thing people ask me about is if they may continue living in the home during the sale. I suggest you ask the estate sale company you hire. It is much easier for you to have moved out and taken everything you want so what is left may be sold. Be sure to also inquire if the company has a minimum charge and what they do regarding contents that are left over at the home. Some clients ask me if they may be present at the home during the sale. That is a question you should ask the company you select.

I do want to make you aware that people shopping an estate sale may make comments on your loved one's home or contents. They are not meant to hurt, but it is also not fun to listen if people criticize choices your loved one has made. Remember that these people are not aware that you have a connection to the home when they are making statements. This is a good reason to not be present at an estate sale.

Here is a success story from an estate sale:

An estate sale we assisted with had a large collection of military items from World War I. We consulted with a local museum and were able to have a story on the news. The day of the sale, there was a line out the door of people who had started lining up around midnight. It was a very successful sale with unique things; however, usable items may sell great too.

Online Estate Sale

An online estate sale works well when you want to control the amount of people coming in and out of your home. A company that conducts an online estate sale will take pictures of items that are to be sold. They then post the items online to sell and set a day and time that the doors to the home will be open for people to pick up items they purchased at the online sale. This option is good if you prefer to not have people walking throughout your loved one's home to purchase items. The downside is that it might be more difficult to sell the smaller items, and you may be left with quite a bit to clear out of the home.

Estate Buyout

Depending on what you are selling and the market for those items, sometimes an estate sale company may offer to do a buyout. They will offer you an amount to take contents and sell them themselves. Since they will be doing the work themselves, a buyout offer may not be large. If you choose this option, do make sure you know if the person or company offering the buyout will take everything or leave you with the unwanted items to still dispose of yourself. This option may seem best if you are busy and feel like your loved one may not have anything of value, but I suggest you use caution with this option. We have found quite a bit of money, jewelry, guns, and other valuables through the years that family never even knew existed. For example:

We were hired by a trust department to go through a home for a client who had passed away. The home was sparsely decorated, but there was a shed out back with quite a few items. We had to use a wasp fogger to kill the wasps in the shed to gain access to the contents. Once we were able to sort through the items, we found several pieces of gold jewelry. The trust officer told us that every time the deceased gentleman and a girlfriend broke up, he would bag up whatever she left and throw it in the shed. We never know what we will find in a home or detached building.

Auction at the Home

Auctions are more prevalent in certain areas than estate sales. They are a good option too. An auction is when an auctioneer sells contents to the highest bidder the day of the auction. Often, items are grouped and auctioned together. The downside to an auction is that you are limited on sale prices as to who shows up the day of the sale and what they are willing to bid. An exception to this is if a company puts a reserve amount on an item. If the reserve amount is not met, an item may not sell. Keep in mind, you could potentially be charged a commission on that item even if it doesn't sell. If it is an outside auction and there is concern with the weather, it might limit who shows up to bid.

The great thing about an auction is that it should clear all contents and small items from the home usually in one day.

Online Auction

An online auction could be an option similar to an online estate sale. The difference is that a minimum price should be set, and people will then bid the price up on what they want to purchase. This could be a good option for items that are not too large to ship and/or items that people are willing to travel to pick up. Some auctioneers have a worldwide following and could have an audience to sell to that is very expansive.

Auction House

Some communities have an auction house where items may be moved in order to be sold. Weather should be less of a factor than for an on-site auction. Items should be photographed and listed online along with the date and time of the auction. The contents are then bid on by people at the auction in a manner similar to an on-site auction. One of the negatives regarding an auction house is that you must pay to have items moved to the auction house. A positive is that if you are striving to empty a home quickly, then this might be a good option.

Specialized Auction

Sometimes an aging loved one has valuable items such as jewelry, designer clothing, original artwork, or even a classic car that might need to be sold by an auctioneer with a large following that extends out of the area you live in. Search out an auctioneer that has a wide reach in order to get the most amount of money for your item(s).

Consignment Store

A consignment store could be an option for disposing of nice furniture. Consignment stores tend to be located in larger communities. Most of them ask for pictures of what you have to sell and will let you know when a good time is to have it delivered to the store. They should be honest about the market they have for your items and will keep a percentage of what the items sold for in return for their services. Most of the time, they display items nicely, set a price, and reduce the price on a set schedule until the item sells. You will want to ask what percentage they keep from the sale of the item and what they do if an item doesn't sell at all. I've seen consignment stores also sell nice accessories and framed artwork. It will all depend on their market. Most often, you will have to pay to have items moved to a consignment store, but the store may be able to suggest a mover they work closely with if you need that advice.

Swap and Shops/Facebook Marketplace/Craigslist

I have clients who ask me about selling items online. This way of selling items has become very popular recently. I don't routinely recommend this method of selling items to my clients. The reason I do not recommend it is because I personally don't feel comfortable inviting strangers to my home. If you are selling smaller items and can meet the purchaser at a public, preferably indoor, meeting place, it would be safer. Some police departments offer locations for exchanging items for sale in their lobby. Be very careful selling any items of high value or items that would require a person to come to your home.

There are other factors to consider if you decide to sell items yourself on these platforms. For example:

I recently spoke with an associate who sold a sofa sleeper and loveseat on Facebook Marketplace for his parents. The gentleman who showed up came with a trailer but no help. The gentleman I knew had to help move the furniture out of the basement. Along with the safety concern of selling the item is the physical work it may take you to complete the transaction.

Donation

If you have a charity you prefer and they are willing to accept the items your aging loved one no longer needs, donation may be a good option. Consult your tax professional as to if you can take a tax write-off for that donation. One thing that has been recommended to me many times through the years is to donate craft items to assisted living communities and material to churches that may have sewing circles. Please consult those communities and churches in your area for further information. In the Midwest, I have seen churches and pet shelters hold large garage sales with donated items in order to help support their mission. Pet shelters may also be able to use towels and sheets you no longer need.

I recently had a client who had a dress from the Civil War era. The dress had been passed down to her through the family and she displayed it on a dress form in a spare bedroom. Her biggest concern with moving was what she was going to do with that dress. I was able to speak with the executive director of the Missouri Civil War Museum in the St. Louis area. The gentleman and his daughter made a trip to authenticate the dress and pick it up. It was added to their collection at the museum. My client was very happy the dress had a new home and would be enjoyed by the public for years to come.

Trash

The last step in clearing out a home is always having the trash removed. You may be able to put the trash out to be picked up or have someone haul it off. If not, a roll-off dumpster may work if allowed where the home is, or you may call a trash-hauling service.

What you choose to do with the leftover contents from your loved one's home may depend on options available where they live, and it may require a couple of steps. You may sell what you can and then donate the remaining items. Please make sure you have a contract if you decide you would like to work with a company in disposing of your loved one's home contents. It should spell out the rate they are charging, a timeline for when the work is to be completed, a minimum amount of commission if they have one, and if the company and its workers are insured and bonded. You should also ask what a company will do to get rid of the remaining contents after they have a sale.

For you and your loved one's safety, never accept a verbal commitment.

One other item I would like to mention when disposing of contents is clothing. Most of the time clothing needs to be donated. An attempt may be made to sell clothing at a sale, but you must have a person who is the right size, likes the items, and is willing to pay for them. The exception to this is vintage clothing. There are shops that exist that will purchase vintage clothing. Vintage clothing may be described as clothing that is at least twenty years old and representative of a particular era. The best way to locate a vintage seller is through an internet search.

Please remember that the contents in a loved one's home were not accumulated overnight and will not be gone overnight either. It is a process and will take time.

CHAPTER 8

Suggestions and Items You Should Be Careful in Handling

As you sort through an aging loved one's contents, there are a few things you should be cautious in handling.

Documents

Many people hold on to old bank statements, tax returns, checks, and miscellaneous paperwork. Frequently, *older documents have an individual's social security number* on them. Any items with personal information should be *shredded* to keep their identity safe. Shredding services can be found at some local stores, banks, and local shredding events held in communities. There are also some companies that focus on shredding. Some of them allow you to drop off your shredding, and some pick up shredding from your location.

Pictures

Pictures are another item that are frequently found in an estate. An option for handling pictures is to have them scanned to an external hard drive or a thumb drive. Here's one way my company handled this for a client:

We helped with an estate where three adult children needed to split up family pictures. The most efficient way we found to do that was to have pictures scanned, and each person received an external hard drive. We did remove and scan pictures from frames—even large photos.

Artwork

Artwork is an item that requires reviewing. It may be difficult to know if the artwork in the home is valuable. It may be best to consult with an art specialist, and those may be found online. While it's unlikely that most artwork will have value, it is possible:

I recently worked with a client clearing out her mother's home. In a storage area in the home, she found an authentic Andy Warhol painting! An art specialist confirmed the authenticity of the piece. The family was having an estate sale at the home but decided to hold on to the painting.

Medications

Prescription and over-the-counter medication disposal should be handled very carefully. Many police departments and several pharmacies will accept any medications to incinerate them. They do not accept sharp items such as needles. Disposing of medication has become even more important to keep the medications from being abused as well as to keep them out of the water supply. The government does offer National Prescription Take Back days periodically. Remember to remove personal information from the prescriptions.

Large, Valuable Items

Safely transporting large, valuable items could be completed by having a crate built around the item. This is frequently done with artwork, irreplaceable antiques, and other highly valuable items. The best way to find a local company to complete this is to search the internet.

Hazardous Substances

Oil, paint, and other hazardous substances should be disposed of at a center that recycles such items. I would suggest searching the internet for a recycling center near you.

Books

Books are items that some people have quite a few of in their home. There are stores that may purchase books from you, but you may also consider donating them to a local library, school, or assisted living community.

Pet Supplies

Pet supplies that are still usable may be donated to a local pet shelter or pet rescue. These include items such as cages, beds, bedding, toys, food, old towels, sheets, and blankets. Shelters are grateful for donations.

Items Being Moved a Long Distance

You may have items that need to be shipped across the country. Package them well, and then obtain quotes from shipping companies, and, if the items are large, from freight companies as to the cost of shipping.

CHAPTER 9

Hoarding

Compulsive hoarding or hoarding disorder is a behavioral or mental disorder and is much more prevalent than people realize. People who hoard feel a need to acquire and hold on to items even if they are useless. Hoarders may become physically ill if you try to get them to part with items.

The concern with hoarding is that the home may become unsafe to reside in. Intervention by a family member to encourage someone to get rid of items can be useless and cause a rift. I've seen where hoarding is prevalent within families. Frequently, there is a reason why people hoard. It may be that they grew up with a parent who saved everything "just in case" they could use it in the future. Plastic containers, foil, cardboard boxes, and newspapers are examples of what I see. Food is also another item people hoard. Some clients we have worked with have items that require refrigeration, but they leave them out on the counter because their refrigerator is full of old food. Much of that food is not safe for them to consume and may make them sick if they do consume it. I've encountered three memorable hoarders over the past few years:

One hoarder lived in a small community outside Kansas City. Walking into her home was like walking back into the 1970s. She saved every wrapper, plastic food container, and magazine. In fact, she never paid for trash service. She slept in the basement when it was hot so she didn't have to use her air conditioner. She also used a bucket and threw her waste outside to save on water usage. Ironically, we found thousands of dollars hidden in the home in drawers, in laundry hampers, between mattresses, and more.

Another client lived at an assisted living community and would sneak out at night to bring the recycling items from her floor back to her apartment. This became a problem because too many things in her apartment made it a fall hazard for her. She wouldn't let the housekeepers in to clean and that resulted in a bug infestation in her apartment. Ultimately, she had to be placed in an apartment where she received additional care and was kept closely watched.

The other hoarder had built on to their home twice to house their collection of more than 100,000 record albums. Unfortunately, some of the records had warped and were useless. The other problem with records was the weight. They were heavy, and that had resulted in cracks in the ceiling beside the support beams. We were able to locate an estate sale company who held multiple sales by setting up tents in the yard and pulling items out to the tents. It took several weeks, but the home eventually was cleaned out. This client moved from her home after she had fallen among all of the clutter, and the home was deemed uninhabitable.

As much as I would like to say it's an easy process to work through the issues and the home, it usually isn't. It would be much better to hire a trustworthy company to help with the job. Please remember that the cost to clear out the home will, most likely, exceed the amount of what is sold. As mentioned before, if necessary, please involve your aging loved one's doctor and/or request someone be a guardian for them.

CHAPTER 10

The Family Home

Now that the home is empty or almost empty, what do you do next? Some homes are in excellent condition and, with a good cleaning, are ready to be put on the market. Others may show signs of delayed maintenance and are not considered to be move-in ready. *How much do you want to invest in updates and/or repairs?* As you may have heard, kitchens and bathrooms should generate the most value when updating, but do you really need to complete the updating? That all depends on the current market, how quickly you would like to sell, and what amount you would like to generate when selling the home.

We have all heard of the options of selling a home "as is" to companies. You only need to watch TV for a short time to see how many of these companies exist today. There is obviously money in buying a home and fixing it up for resale. Along with these companies, many people like to "flip" homes. The goal of these companies and individuals is to buy cheap and then sell for a profit. That being said, you can probably guess that the offer to purchase may be low. Here is one experience from a client:

I had a client who was offered $40,000 for their home. The home was outdated and needed flooring and windows replaced. My client's son was very handy and invested approximately $25,000 doing repairs and updates to the home. We were able to sell that home for $170,000.

The best way to get the most out of the property is to either look for the person who wants to live there themselves or make a few necessary repairs and/or updates in order to profit from the home sale yourself.

Whatever option you choose, ask many questions about what you will ultimately receive from the sale of the home. Enlisting the help of a licensed Realtor would be a great option for you. They will have the ability to help you set a price for the home, market the home, and complete the necessary paperwork in a timely manner. There are strict timelines for paperwork in real estate. If you miss those deadlines, you could jeopardize the sale of the home.

Realtors that belong to the local Multiple Listing Service (MLS) will be able to market your property to other brokers/Realtors to help sell the home. The MLS is a database that provides information to other Realtors who may have a client interested in purchasing your home. A Realtor will also be able to establish an asking price for your home by analyzing comparable home sales in the area. The Realtor will compare location, condition, and square footage and determine if updates are needed in establishing a price for your home.

A home that is priced correctly *will* sell in a timely manner. A home that is overpriced may stay on the market for a long time. Ultimately, people may wonder why the home is on the market so long, and you could potentially end up with a lower offer than if you had priced it correctly.

In a seller's market, a home priced correctly may generate multiple offers. If that is the case, you would need to compare the offers to see which one is the strongest. By strongest, I don't only mean the most amount of money being offered. The terms, the type of loan, whether will you be required to complete additional repairs, the closing date, and the closing costs required to be paid by the seller are some of the things you should consider when comparing offers. Certain loan types will require you to complete additional repairs prior to closing. These are a few of the items a Realtor will guide you through and why hiring one is well worth the fee.

What other options might exist for the family home? You may decide to keep the home. For example:

My father chose to do that with his parents' family home. In this case, you could manage the property, rent collection, repairs, and so forth on your own or hire a management company. Management companies charge a fee to do just that—manage concerns with the property.

My husband is from a small town in Iowa. In that community, family members sometimes choose to keep the family home for a weekend getaway. If you choose an option similar to this, you will need to come to an agreement as to how bills and repairs on the property will be divided between the new owners.

What about the option of auctioning a home? Many auction companies prefer the option to auction a home if they are selling the contents too. They should be able to discuss details with you and set a reserve to guarantee that you receive a certain amount from the sale if you choose this option.

CHAPTER 11

Pertinent Information and Seeking Legal Advice

Moving an aging loved one is complex, and it can involve many sensitive issues, including paperwork, assets, and more. You might need to seek an attorney for legal advice, and before you begin to downsize your aging loved one, someone should be aware of their assets. You should organize your loved one's pertinent information in a binder before or during the moving process to avoid it being lost or trashed.

Legal Documents to Identify and Organize

Legal documents are state specific:

- A **will** is a legal document that states a person's wishes and instructions for managing and distributing their estate after death.

- A **trust**, generally speaking, is a relationship in which one person holds the title to property, subject to an obligation to keep or use the property for the benefit of the maker of the trust and possible heirs and others. There are several types of trusts to consider. You should consult with an attorney regarding your specific situation.

Here are a couple of options for titling assets:

- **Transfer on death** generally applies to brokerage accounts, stocks, bonds, and vehicles.

- **Payable on death** generally applies to bank accounts.

Please seek legal advice to decide how to handle transfer on death and payable on death situations.

You should also check beneficiary designations, including past and present beneficiaries on insurance, pensions, retirement accounts, and other documents.

A **power of attorney** (POA) is for financial and medical needs. There are several types of POAs:

- **Limited POA** is for when you need someone to do things for you for a limited purpose. These documents usually specify a date and time period for the POA.

- **General POA** essentially assigns all of one's powers and rights to someone else and terminates with incapacity.

- **Durable POA** lasts even if the assignor becomes incapacitated, unlike the general POA. These durable POAs can be for business (asset management) or health.

- **Springing POA** serves roughly the same purpose as a durable POA, but it only comes into effect once a specific event happens, such as when the assignor becomes incapacitated.

A **living will** is a written, legal document that spells out medical treatments a person would and would not want to be used to keep them alive as well as their preferences for other medical decisions.

An **advance directive** is a legal document that provides instructions for medical care and only goes into effect if your loved one cannot communicate their own wishes. It is a form of a durable POA.

Do not resuscitate tells emergency responders and other health care providers to not perform cardiopulmonary resuscitation (CPR) if your loved one's heart stops (called cardiac arrest) or they stop breathing.

Additional Items to Review or Consider

- Long-term care insurance
- Medical insurance

- Car insurance

- Homeowner's insurance

- Stocks and bonds

- Other investments, such as mutual funds

- Retirement accounts

- Pensions

- Bank accounts

- Car titles

- Tax documents

- Safe deposit boxes—where they are located and where a key may be located

People can be very private, but this is information that someone needs to know. If not you, then it would be good for an attorney to have the information.

In addition, it would be good to have the following:

- Medical history

- Names and phone numbers for your loved one's attorney, accountant, and financial planner

- Doctor's name, location, and phone number

- Social security number

- Prepaid funeral arrangements

- Additional person named on the lockbox

- Credit card information so they may be cancelled

- Login information for accounts

Be aware of these items and be proactive to prevent problems from occurring. Some items may be placed in a trust, and some may be transfer on death and payable on death situations.

As mentioned earlier, please consult an attorney for legal advice.

CHAPTER 12

How Clear It Out
Handles the Process

My company, Clear It Out, handles the situations described in this book, making the process of moving your aged loved one a bit easier. Here is how we do it:

1. We offer a free consultation where we discuss your goals, timeline, the client's new residence, and how many of their possessions they can and want to take with them. This is also when the discussion happens regarding the home, contents, and what they and you would like to do with them.

2. We pack for the move and schedule the move with a trusted partner.

3. We help the client get unpacked and settled.

4. We address the items left over. Would the client like to have an estate sale, to sell off the most valuable contents and donate the remaining, or to do a combination of both?

5. We make the necessary connections for the client, such as an estate sale company, auction house, charity, and, if necessary, a trash hauler.

6. We discuss the home and, if necessary, needed repairs or updates to bring a higher selling price.

As for the home, sometimes it is feasible to complete repairs to bring a higher selling price. However, some clients prefer to sell as-is. There is not a right or wrong answer because every situation is different.

Conclusion

The process for someone needing to downsize and move is different for everyone. It can be emotionally draining, from making the decision that a loved one is no longer able to care effectively for themselves or their residence to what to do with all of their possessions. Most everything they have collected through the years has a memory associated with it. At times, tears may be shed—both happy and sad tears. It is all part of the process.

Be gentle but encouraging while going through the process. Frequently, it may be best to hire an outside company to help. This allows family to enjoy time together and not feel the pressure to "accomplish" a task every time they get together. Remember it is best to start early and take small steps. Your loved one did not accumulate the things they own in a day and they won't be gone that quick either. You will get there!

Resource for Help

For assistance with the process where you live, please email Jennifer Taylor at:

Jennifer@ClearItOutKC.com

Jennifer's team can research options where you live and provide contact information.

About the Author

Jennifer Taylor of Kansas City, Missouri, is a successful entrepreneur and Realtor specializing in helping seniors and their families with downsizing and moving. Jennifer graduated from Benedictine College with a bachelor of arts in business administration and from Mid-America Nazarene University with a master of business administration. After graduating from college and before starting Clear It Out, Jennifer was a flight attendant and worked as a financial analyst and underwriter for a major insurance company. Jennifer does speaking engagements throughout her community, providing tips to make the downsizing and moving process go smoother and to help people get started.

Jennifer and her husband, Todd, have been married for more than thirty years and are the parents to three wonderful children, including a set of twins. She founded Clear It Out while raising her young family, as she wanted a career that helped people and that was on her own schedule so she could be involved in her children's activities. Later, as her children grew up, she became a Realtor to provide even broader services to clients.

After helping hundreds of clients with Clear It Out, Jennifer has learned the most efficient ways to get the project of downsizing and moving accomplished while realizing that each client's needs are different both regarding their possessions and emotions. As with everything in life, Jennifer believes you should take the process one day at a time and not worry too much about things that can be fixed or accomplished even if they may seem to be a big deal at the moment.

To learn more about Jennifer's business, visit her website ClearItOutKC.com.

www.ingramcontent.com/pod-product-compliance
Lightning Source LLC
Chambersburg PA
CBHW061709120626
46550CB00003B/1159